DINOSAUR Academy

Times Tables

ARCTURUS

Key skills in this book

ARCTURUS

This edition published in 2023 by Arcturus Publishing Limited
26/27 Bickels Yard, 151–153 Bermondsey Street,
London SE1 3HA

Author: Lisa Regan
Illustrator: Claire Stamper
Editors: Donna Gregory and Lucy Doncaster
Designer: Linda Storey
Design Manager: Jessica Holliland
Managing Editor: Joe Harris

ISBN: 978-1-3988-2196-5
CH010834NT
Supplier 29, Date 0523, PI 00003155

Printed in China

Introduction

Welcome to the Dinosaur Academy! Join the dinosaurs and their prehistoric friends as they set out to discover just how terrific times tables can be.

In this book, you'll find lots of fun activities that will help you learn and perfect your times tables. Start at the beginning, where you will learn the basics with the two, ten, and five times tables, and then work through the book right up to the twelve times table. There are loads of awesome activities to help you improve and give you confidence—even with big numbers. So, grab your pencil, put on your thinking cap, and let's get going!

 # Groups of two

Each Torosaurus has two large horns. Write the total number of horns for each group of dinosaurs. The first has been done to help you.

 1 two-horned Torosaurus = **2** horns

 2 two-horned Torosaurus = horns

 3 two-horned Torosaurus = horns

 4 two-horned Torosaurus = horns

 5 two-horned Torosaurus = horns

 6 two-horned Torosaurus = horns

More twos

Now try it with these two-horned dinosaurs.

7 two-horned Torosaurus = [ ] horns

8 two-horned Torosaurus = [ ] horns

9 two-horned Torosaurus = [ ] horns

10 two-horned Torosaurus = [ ] horns

Repeated addition

The flying reptiles have flocked together.
Can you count up how many there are in each group,
using your addition and multiplication skills?

     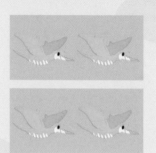 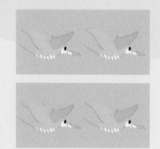

2 + 2 + 2 = ☐   2 + 2 + 2 + 2 = ☐

3 x 2 = ☐   4 x 2 = ☐

    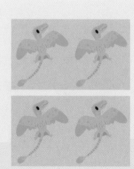 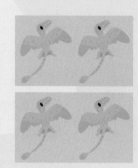 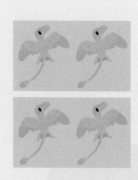

2 + 2 = ☐   2 + 2 + 2 + 2 + 2 + 2 = ☐

2 x 2 = ☐   6 x 2 = ☐

Match up

Help Brandon the Brachiosaurus join each addition fact to the dot with the correct multiplication fact on it. The first one has been done for you.

6×2

$2 + 2 + 2 + 2 + 2 + 2 + 2$

3×2

$2 + 2 + 2 + 2 + 2$

4×2

$2 + 2 + 2 + 2 + 2 + 2$

$2 + 2 + 2$

5×2

$2 + 2 + 2 + 2$

7×2

Number lines

Use the number lines to solve the multiplication problems, like the first example. Circle the answers.

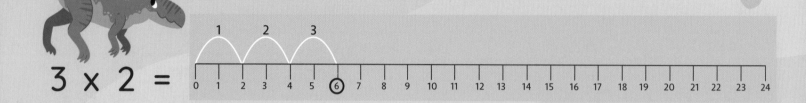

$3 \times 2 =$

1 2 3

0 1 2 3 4 5 ⑥ 7 8 9 10 11 12 13 14 15 16 17 18 19 20 21 22 23 24

$5 \times 2 =$

1

0 1 2 3 4 5 6 7 8 9 10 11 12 13 14 15 16 17 18 19 20 21 22 23 24

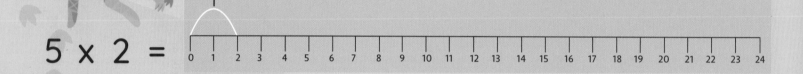

$8 \times 2 =$

1

0 1 2 3 4 5 6 7 8 9 10 11 12 13 14 15 16 17 18 19 20 21 22 23 24

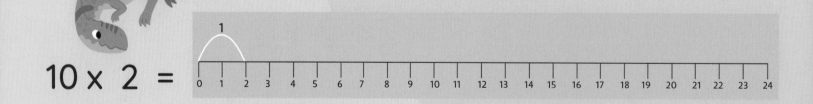

$10 \times 2 =$

1

0 1 2 3 4 5 6 7 8 9 10 11 12 13 14 15 16 17 18 19 20 21 22 23 24

Rock hoppers

Help the little Eoraptors get to the grown-up by hopping across the rocks. A hops on every second rock; B jumps on every third rock; C leaps on every fourth rock.

Two times table

Two more pterosaurs turn up at the lake every hour.
How many will there be after 12 hours?

1 x 2 =

2 x 2 =

3 x 2 =

4 x 2 =

5 x 2 =

6 x 2 =

7 x 2 =

8 x 2 =

9 x 2 =

10 x 2 =

11 x 2 =

12 x 2 =

Missing numbers

Follow the example to write which times tables problems these groups of dino-friends are making.

3 pairs: 3 x 2 = 6

5 pairs: ☐ x ☐ = ☐

4 pairs: ☐ x ☐ = ☐

2 pairs: ☐ x ☐ = ☐

6 pairs: ☐ x ☐ = ☐

Matching multiples

Each fossil contains a multiple of two. Can you match the correct one to each problem?

6

12 x 2

6 x 2

8 x 2

14

3 x 2

18

11 x 2

4 x 2

16

24

9 x 2

7 x 2

12

22

8

What's missing?

Help the friends work out which numbers are needed to fill in the blanks.

$3 \times \boxed{} = 6$ $8 \times 2 = \boxed{}$

$7 \times 2 = \boxed{}$ $\boxed{} \times 2 = 2$

$\boxed{} \times 2 = 10$ $\boxed{} \times 2 = 18$

$\boxed{} \times 2 = 20$ $2 \times 2 = \boxed{}$

$4 \times 2 = \boxed{}$ $6 \times 2 = \boxed{}$

Groups of ten

Each of these stylish Stegosaurus has 10 back plates.
How many do they have when they get together?

2 stylish Stegosaurus $10 + 10 =$ ☐ $2 \times 10 =$ ☐

4 stylish Stegosaurus $10 + 10 + 10 + 10 =$ ☐

$4 \times 10 =$ ☐

6 stylish Stegosaurus $10 + 10 + 10 + 10 + 10 + 10 =$ ☐

$6 \times 10 =$ ☐

More fossils

Use the number lines to solve these problems. Write the answers in the boxes. The first one has been done for you.

2 x 10 = **20**

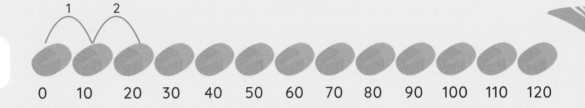

0 10 20 30 40 50 60 70 80 90 100 110 120

5 x 10 =

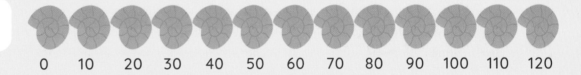

0 10 20 30 40 50 60 70 80 90 100 110 120

10 x 10 =

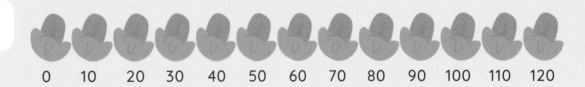

0 10 20 30 40 50 60 70 80 90 100 110 120

6 x 10 =

0 10 20 30 40 50 60 70 80 90 100 110 120

Ten times table

Each mega-reptile can scoop up 10 fish in one mouthful.
How many fish are contained in 12 mouthfuls?

$1 \times 10 =$ ☐

$2 \times 10 =$ ☐

$3 \times 10 =$ ☐

$4 \times 10 =$ ☐

$5 \times 10 =$ ☐

$6 \times 10 =$ ☐

$7 \times 10 =$ ☐

$8 \times 10 =$ ☐

$9 \times 10 =$ ☐

$10 \times 10 =$ ☐

$11 \times 10 =$ ☐

$12 \times 10 =$ ☐

Missing numbers

These crested dinosaurs need your help.
Can you fill in all of the missing numbers?

$1 \times \boxed{} = 10$　　　　$10 \times \boxed{} = 100$

$\boxed{} \times 10 = 90$　　　　$5 \times 10 = \boxed{}$

$2 \times 10 = \boxed{}$　　　　$\boxed{} \times 10 = 80$

$11 \times \boxed{} = 110$　　　　$7 \times 10 = \boxed{}$

$\boxed{} \times 10 = 30$　　　　$\boxed{} \times 10 = 120$

$6 \times 10 = \boxed{}$　　　　$4 \times 10 = \boxed{}$

Heads and tails

Write in the missing tail numbers by multiplying the head numbers by the body numbers. The first one has been done for you.

Flying high

Find a path through the Ornithocheirus,
following them in the order of the 10 times table.

Dot to dot

Help Dorothy the Diplodocus join each addition fact
to the dot with the correct multiplication fact on it.

10 + 10 + 10 + 10 + 10 + 10 + 10 + 10

5 x 10

4 x 10

10 + 10 + 10 + 10

8 x 10

10 + 10 + 10 + 10 + 10

10 + 10 + 10 + 10 + 10 + 10 + 10 + 10 + 10 + 10 + 10

3 x 10

11 x 10

10 + 10 + 10

Pick a partner

Help the dinosaurs choose their dance partners by matching them up.

40

8 x 10

7 x 10

90

70

5 x 10

4 x 10

50

60

6 x 10

80

9 x 10

21

Groups of five

Each nest contains five eggs. Can you count up how many eggs there are in each group, using your addition and multiplication skills?

2 nests containing 5 eggs each

$5 + 5 =$ ☐ $2 \times 5 =$ ☐

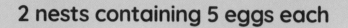

4 nests containing 5 eggs each

$5 + 5 + 5 + 5 =$ ☐ $4 \times 5 =$ ☐

10 nests containing 5 eggs each

$5 + 5 + 5 + 5 + 5 + 5 + 5 + 5 + 5 + 5 =$ ☐

$10 \times 5 =$ ☐

Even dinos love their toys

Circle all the toy bears that have numbers that are multiples of 5.
Remember, all the answers in the five times table end in 5 or 0.

Five times table

These Allosaurus are counting caterpillars and sorting them into groups of five. Help them count how many there are in total for each group.

1 x 5 = ☐   7 x 5 = ☐

2 x 5 = ☐   8 x 5 = ☐

3 x 5 = ☐   9 x 5 = ☐

4 x 5 = ☐   10 x 5 = ☐

5 x 5 = ☐   11 x 5 = ☐

6 x 5 = ☐   12 x 5 = ☐

Missing numbers

Draw lines to match each dinosaur with the food it likes best.

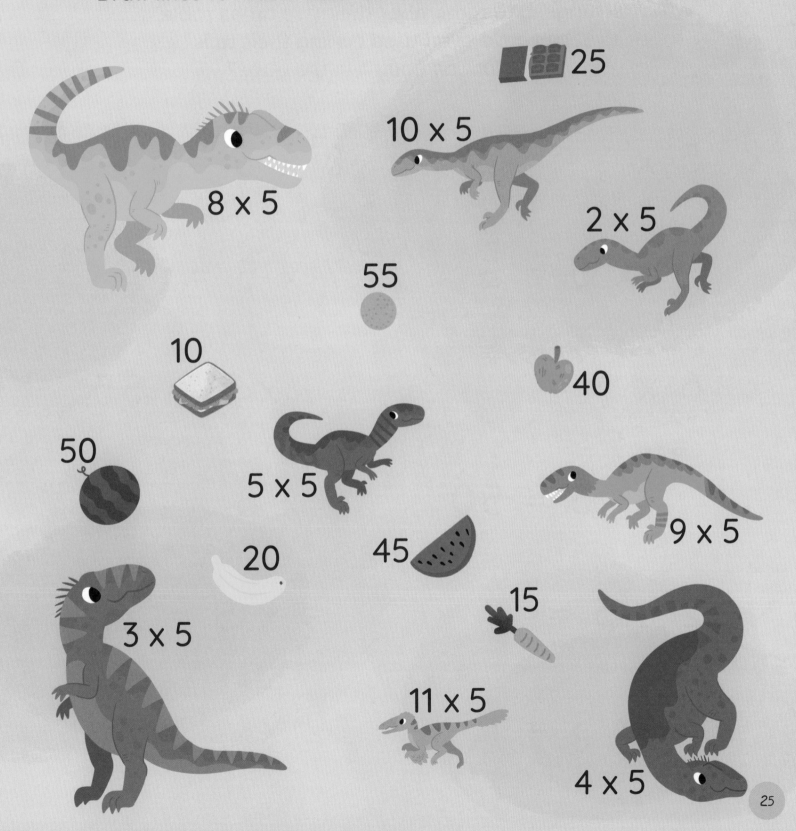

25

10 x 5

8 x 5

2 x 5

55

10

40

50

5 x 5

9 x 5

20

45

15

3 x 5

11 x 5

4 x 5

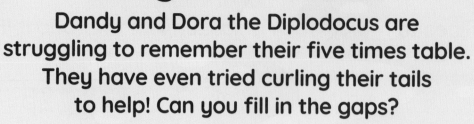

Forgetful fives

Dandy and Dora the Diplodocus are
struggling to remember their five times table.
They have even tried curling their tails
to help! Can you fill in the gaps?

5 x ☐ = 25   8 x 5 = ☐

☐ x 5 = 5   7 x 5 = ☐

6 x 5 = ☐   ☐ x 5 = 55

☐ x 5 = 50   9 x 5 = ☐

2 x 5 = ☐   ☐ x 5 = 20

☐ x 5 = 15   12 x ☐ = 60

High five

Ignatius the Iguanodon is working on his five times table.
Fill in all the missing answers to help him.

$1 \times 5 = \boxed{}$

$7 \times 5 = \boxed{}$

$2 \times 5 = \boxed{}$

$8 \times 5 = \boxed{}$

$3 \times 5 = \boxed{}$

$9 \times 5 = \boxed{}$

$4 \times 5 = \boxed{}$

$10 \times 5 = \boxed{}$

$11 \times 5 = \boxed{}$

$5 \times 5 = \boxed{}$

$12 \times 5 = \boxed{}$

$6 \times 5 = \boxed{}$

Groups of four

The dinosaurs are collecting flowers. If each collects four flowers, how many do they collect altogether?

2 dinosaurs pick 4 flowers each

4 + 4 = ☐   2 x 4 = ☐

3 dinosaurs pick 4 flowers each

4 + 4 + 4 = ☐   3 x 4 = ☐

5 dinosaurs pick 4 flowers each

4 + 4 + 4 + 4 + 4 = ☐

5 x 4 = ☐

Darting dragonflies

Circle every fourth dragonfly until you reach the sleeping dinosaur at the bottom.

Four times table

Each Ankylosaurus has four legs. Work out how many legs there are as more join the group.

1 x 4 =

2 x 4 =

3 x 4 =

4 x 4 =

5 x 4 =

6 x 4 =

7 x 4 =

8 x 4 =

9 x 4 =

10 x 4 =

11 x 4 =

12 x 4 =

Missing numbers

Help the clever dinosaur fill in the gaps in these problems.

$6 \times \boxed{} = 24$ $\boxed{} \times 4 = 44$

$10 \times 4 = \boxed{}$ $7 \times 4 = \boxed{}$

$\boxed{} \times 4 = 16$ $5 \times \boxed{} = 20$

$9 \times 4 = \boxed{}$ $\boxed{} \times 4 = 32$

$\boxed{} \times 4 = 4$ $3 \times 4 = \boxed{}$

$2 \times \boxed{} = 8$ $\boxed{} \times 4 = 48$

Deep thinkers

Work out the answer to each problem and
write it in the thought bubble.

4 x 4 =

7 x 4 =

5 x 4 =

9 x 4 =

10 x 4 =

3 x 4 =

Something's wrong

One of the Lambeosaurus has got muddled, and doesn't have a number from the four times table. Which one is it?

Groups of eight

This sauropod eats eight leaves in one mouthful.
How many leaves does she munch in more mouthfuls?

2 mouthfuls of 8 leaves

$8 + 8 =$ ☐ $2 \times 8 =$ ☐

3 mouthfuls of 8 leaves

$8 + 8 + 8 =$ ☐ $3 \times 8 =$ ☐

5 mouthfuls of 8 leaves

$8 + 8 + 8 + 8 + 8 =$ ☐ $5 \times 8 =$ ☐

9 mouthfuls of 8 leaves

$8 + 8 + 8 + 8 + 8 + 8 + 8 + 8 + 8 =$ ☐

$9 \times 8 =$ ☐

Lost and found

Help the mother Styracosaurus find her babies by following the path. Fill in the missing multiples from the eight times table on the way, in the correct order.

8

16

32

72

56

Eight times table

How many legs are there on
each collection of octopuses?

1 x 8 = ☐

2 x 8 = ☐

3 x 8 = ☐

4 x 8 = ☐

5 x 8 = ☐

6 x 8 = ☐

7 x 8 = ☐

8 x 8 = ☐

9 x 8 = ☐

10 x 8 = ☐

11 x 8 = ☐

12 x 8 = ☐

Missing numbers

Some numbers from these equations in the eight times table have been washed away by the tide. Can you fill them in?

$1 \times \boxed{} = 8$

$\boxed{} \times 8 = 24$

$\boxed{} \times 8 = 64$

$6 \times 8 = \boxed{}$

$5 \times 8 = \boxed{}$

$\boxed{} \times 8 = 56$

$9 \times \boxed{} = 72$

$11 \times 8 = \boxed{}$

$\boxed{} \times 8 = 80$

$\boxed{} \times 8 = 32$

$2 \times 8 = \boxed{}$

$12 \times 8 = \boxed{}$

Broom broom!

It's race day, and each dinosaur must find a car to push. Draw lines to match them up.

40

11 x 8

32

4 x 8

2 x 8

88

56

5 x 8

9 x 8

7 x 8

16

72

38

Crazy creatures

First, solve each sum and write the answer on the dot. Next, follow the key to shade in the dinosaurs.

- 1 x 8
- 2 x 8
- 3 x 8
- 4 x 8
- 5 x 8
- 6 x 8

39

Groups of three

If the little Rhamphorhynchus play by the trees in groups of three, work out how many there are each time.

2 trees with 3 flying friends

$3 + 3 =$ ☐ $2 \times 3 =$ ☐

3 trees with 3 flying friends

$3 + 3 + 3 =$ ☐ $3 \times 3 =$ ☐

5 trees with 3 flying friends

$3 + 3 + 3 + 3 + 3 =$ ☐ $5 \times 3 =$ ☐

6 trees with 3 flying friends

$3 + 3 + 3 + 3 + 3 + 3 =$ ☐

$6 \times 3 =$ ☐

Forest trail

Help Annie the Ankylosaurus through the forest by following a route that passes through numbers in the three times table, in the correct order.

41

Three times table

If a pterosaur flies for three hours each day, for how long do they fly in a week? How long in 12 days? Fill in the three times table to work it out!

1 x 3 =

2 x 3 =

3 x 3 =

4 x 3 =

5 x 3 =

6 x 3 =

7 x 3 =

8 x 3 =

9 x 3 =

 10 x 3 =

11 x 3 =

12 x 3 =

Missing numbers

Help these flyers fill in the missing numbers from the three times table.

[ ] x 3 = 3

6 x 3 = [ ]

10 x [ ] = 30

[ ] x 3 = 6

5 x 3 = [ ]

[ ] x 3 = 33

3 x 3 = [ ]

[ ] x 3 = 21

9 x 3 = [ ]

4 x 3 = [ ]

[ ] x 3 = 24

12 x 3 = [ ]

Heads and tails

Write in the missing tail numbers by multiplying the head numbers by the body numbers.

4 × 3

10 × 3

× 3

11

× 3

× 3

5

12

6 × 3

9

1 × 3

× 3

× 3

2

7

× 3

3

× 3

8

× 3

Starfall

This curious dinosaur has found some fallen stars. Most of them have numbers from the three times table, but one is wrong. Which one is it?

33

36

30

27

20

15

3

12

24

6

9

Groups of six

The dinosaurs are catching fish. If each catches six fish, how many do they catch in total?

2 dinosaurs catch 6 fish each

$6 + 6 =$ ☐ $2 \times 6 =$ ☐

4 dinosaurs catch 6 fish each

$6 + 6 + 6 + 6 =$ ☐ $4 \times 6 =$ ☐

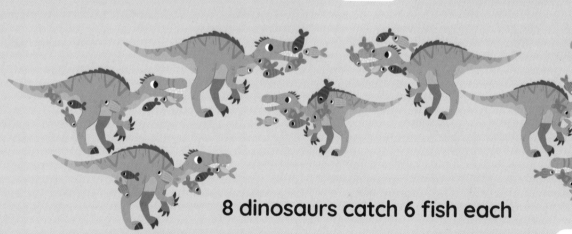

8 dinosaurs catch 6 fish each

$6 + 6 + 6 + 6 + 6 + 6 + 6 + 6 =$ ☐

$8 \times 6 =$ ☐

All the sixes

Each dinosaur has six spots. How many spots are there in each group of dinos? The first one has been done for you.

$$4 \times 6 = 24$$

Six times table

If this dinosaur eats six pieces of fruit each day,
how many will it eat in 12 days?

1 x 6 =

2 x 6 =

3 x 6 =

4 x 6 =

5 x 6 =

6 x 6 =

7 x 6 =

8 x 6 =

9 x 6 =

10 x 6 =

11 x 6 =

12 x 6 =

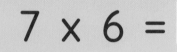

Number square

Every number from the six times table on this number square has been blanked out. Can you fill in the answers?

1	2	3	4	5		7	8	9	10
11		13	14	15	16	17		19	20
21	22	23		25	26	27	28	29	
31	32	33	34	35		37	38	39	40
41		43	44	45	46	47		49	50
51	52	53		55	56	57	58	59	
61	62	63	64	65		67	68	69	70
71		73	74	75	76	77		79	80
81	82	83		85	86	87	88	89	
91	92	93	94	95		97	98	99	100

Missing numbers

Help the speedy dinosaurs fill in the missing numbers. Be as quick as you can!

$1 \times \boxed{} = 6$ $11 \times 6 = \boxed{}$

$6 \times 6 = \boxed{}$ $\boxed{} \times 6 = 54$

$\boxed{} \times 6 = 24$ $7 \times 6 = \boxed{}$

$10 \times \boxed{} = 60$ $\boxed{} \times 6 = 12$

$5 \times 6 = \boxed{}$ $3 \times 6 = \boxed{}$

$\boxed{} \times 6 = 48$ $\boxed{} \times 6 = 72$

Find a friend

Match up the dinosaurs with sums on them to the correct answers.

36

2 x 6

7 x 6

24

48

12

3 x 6

4 x 6

6 x 6

18

42

5 x 6

8 x 6

30

Groups of nine

The little dinosaur gobbles down worms,
nine at a time. Work out how many worms he eats.

2 groups of 9 worms

$$9 + 9 = \boxed{} \qquad 2 \times 9 = \boxed{}$$

4 groups of 9 worms

$$9 + 9 + 9 + 9 = \boxed{} \qquad 4 \times 9 = \boxed{}$$

5 groups of 9 worms

$$9 + 9 + 9 + 9 + 9 = \boxed{} \qquad 5 \times 9 = \boxed{}$$

Down in the deep

Three of the numbers on these sea creatures are part of the 3, 6, and 9 times tables. Can you find them?

Nine times table

Help these little Lambeosaurus fill in their nine times table.

1 x 9 = ☐

2 x 9 = ☐

3 x 9 = ☐

4 x 9 = ☐

5 x 9 = ☐

6 x 9 = ☐

7 x 9 = ☐

8 x 9 = ☐

9 x 9 = ☐

10 x 9 = ☐

11 x 9 = ☐

12 x 9 = ☐

Missing numbers

Help this playful dinosaur fill in the missing numbers in the nine times table. How quickly can you do it?

$1 \times \boxed{} = 9$

$6 \times 9 = \boxed{}$

$2 \times 9 = \boxed{}$

$\boxed{} \times 9 = 72$

$\boxed{} \times 9 = 81$

$11 \times 9 = \boxed{}$

$7 \times 9 = \boxed{}$

$\boxed{} \times 9 = 36$

$10 \times \boxed{} = 90$

$5 \times 9 = \boxed{}$

$\boxed{} \times 9 = 27$

$\boxed{} \times 9 = 108$

Newborns

Match each of the baby dinosaurs with the nest where it hatched.

36

3 x 9

18

2 x 9

81

5 x 9

63

54

7 x 9

8 x 9

72

9 x 9

45

27

4 x 9

6 x 9

Number square

All the multiples of nine have been covered
with fossils. Can you fill them in?

1	2	3	4	5	6	7	8		10
11	12	13	14	15	16	17		19	20
21	22	23	24	25	26		28	29	30
31	32	33	34	35		37	38	39	40
41	42	43	44		46	47	48	49	50
51	52	53		55	56	57	58	59	60
61	62		64	65	66	67	68	69	70
71		73	74	75	76	77	78	79	80
	82	83	84	85	86	87	88	89	
91	92	93	94	95	96	97	98		100

Groups of seven

Each of these tasty bugs has seven spots.
How many spots are there in each group?

2 bugs with 7 spots each

7 + 7 = ☐   2 x 7 = ☐

4 bugs with 7 spots each

7 + 7 + 7 + 7 = ☐   4 x 7 = ☐

5 bugs with 7 spots each

7 + 7 + 7 + 7 + 7 = ☐   5 x 7 = ☐

7 bugs with 7 spots each

7 + 7 + 7 + 7 + 7 + 7 + 7 = ☐

7 x 7 = ☐

Off we go!

The dinosaurs are going away for a week!
Below is what they will need for one day. How many
of each item will they need for all seven days?

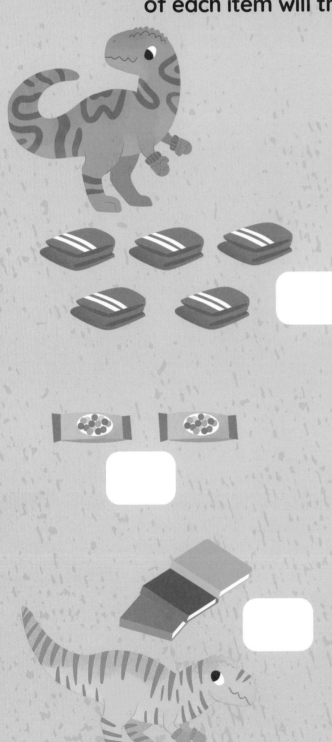

Seven times table

A pterosaur needs to eat seven fish every day. How many fish do four pterosaurs eat? How many do 12 pterosaurs eat?

1 x 7 = ☐

2 x 7 = ☐

3 x 7 = ☐

4 x 7 = ☐

5 x 7 = ☐

6 x 7 = ☐

7 x 7 = ☐

8 x 7 = ☐

9 x 7 = ☐

10 x 7 = ☐

11 x 7 = ☐

12 x 7 = ☐

Missing numbers

Here are some more lovers of fishy snacks.
Can you help them solve the problems?

$1 \times \boxed{} = 7$

$\boxed{} \times 7 = 21$

$10 \times 7 = \boxed{}$

$6 \times 7 = \boxed{}$

$\boxed{} \times 7 = 14$

$\boxed{} \times 7 = 56$

$11 \times \boxed{} = 77$

$4 \times 7 = \boxed{}$

$\boxed{} \times 7 = 35$

$\boxed{} \times 7 = 84$

$9 \times 7 = \boxed{}$

$7 \times 7 = \boxed{}$

Spots and stripes

Match each Allosaurus to the correct footprint.

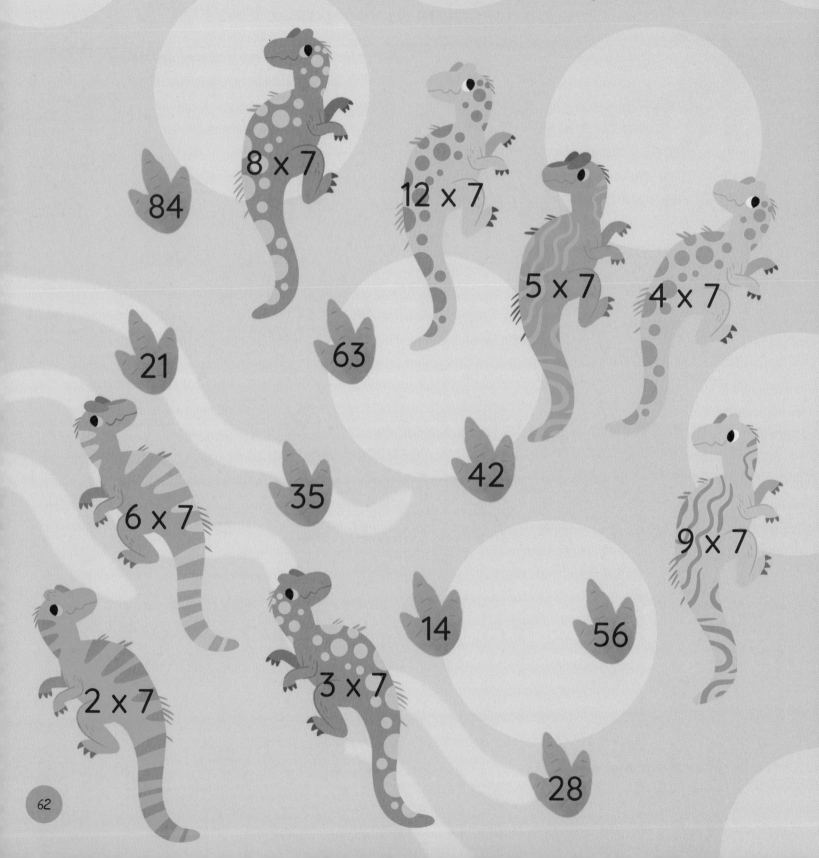

Black and white

First, find a way through the maze, following the seven times table. Then, finish the picture by shading in all of the dinosaurs and pterosaurs.

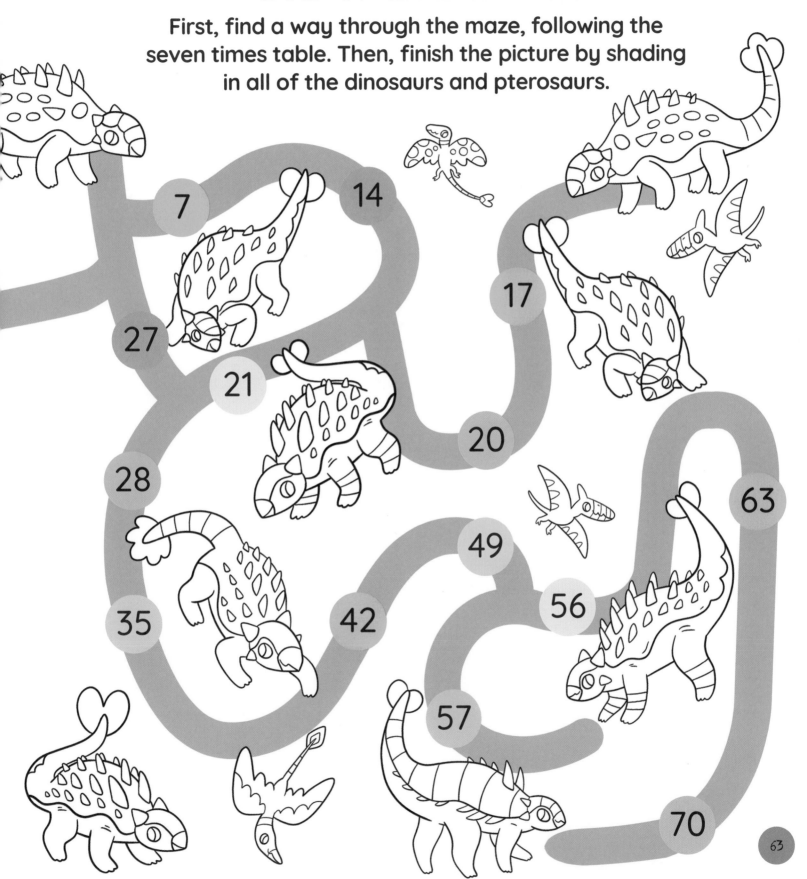

Groups of eleven

It takes 11 ants to carry one large stick.
Work out how many it takes to carry more sticks.

To carry 3 sticks

$11 + 11 + 11 =$ ⬜ $\qquad 3 \times 11 =$ ⬜

To carry 6 sticks

$11 + 11 + 11 + 11 + 11 + 11 =$ ⬜ $\qquad 6 \times 11 =$ ⬜

 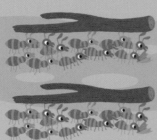  

To carry 8 sticks

$11 + 11 + 11 + 11 + 11 + 11 + 11 + 11 =$ ⬜

$8 \times 11 =$ ⬜

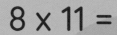

64

All the elevens

Which of the Lambeosaurus has a number that isn't part of the 11 times table?

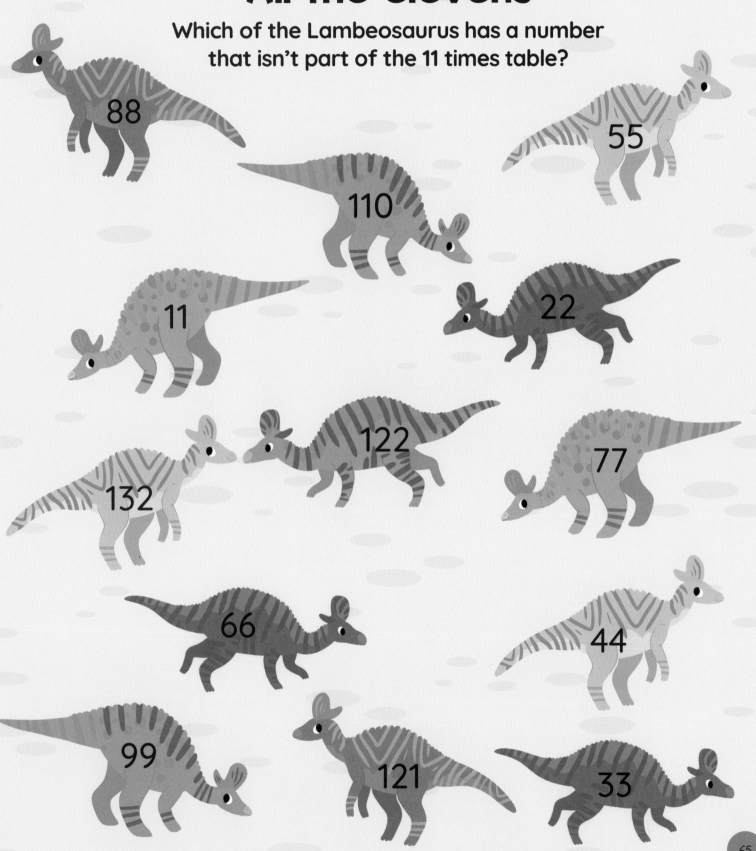

Eleven times table

If a Velociraptor can run 11 miles in a day,
how far can it run over several days?

1 x 11 = ☐

2 x 11 = ☐

3 x 11 = ☐

4 x 11 = ☐

5 x 11 = ☐

6 x 11 = ☐

7 x 11 = ☐

8 x 11 = ☐

9 x 11 = ☐

10 x 11 = ☐

11 x 11 = ☐

12 x 11 = ☐

Missing numbers

Help Violet the Velociraptor to fill in the missing numbers in these equations.

$1 \times \boxed{} = 11$

$2 \times 11 = \boxed{}$

$3 \times 11 = \boxed{}$

$\boxed{} \times 11 = 121$

$\boxed{} \times 11 = 99$

$6 \times 11 = \boxed{}$

$8 \times 11 = \boxed{}$

$\boxed{} \times 11 = 44$

$\boxed{} \times 11 = 55$

$7 \times 11 = \boxed{}$

$10 \times \boxed{} = 110$

$\boxed{} \times 11 = 132$

Practice makes perfect

Theo the Therizinosaurus knows that the best way to learn times tables is to keep doing them over and over. Help fill in the gaps here.

$1 \times 11 =$

$4 \times 11 =$

$10 \times 11 =$

$5 \times 11 =$

$8 \times 11 =$

$7 \times 11 =$

$2 \times 11 =$

$11 \times 11 =$

$9 \times 11 =$

$6 \times 11 =$

$3 \times 11 =$

$12 \times 11 =$

Fancy footwear

Ollie the Ornithocheirus is shopping for a new pair of shoes.
Write the price on the tags by working out the calculations.

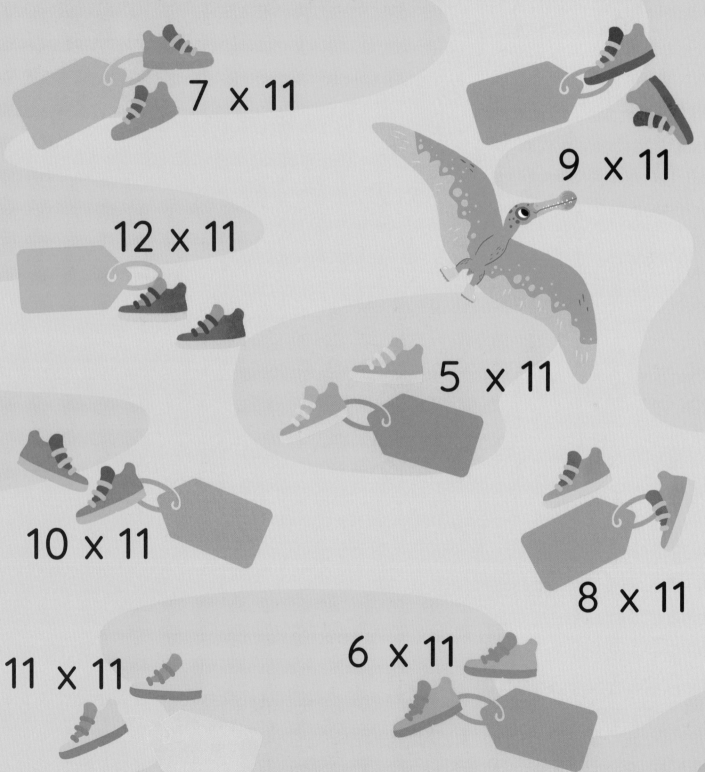

7 x 11

9 x 11

12 x 11

5 x 11

10 x 11

8 x 11

11 x 11

6 x 11

Groups of twelve

These monsters can munch 12 fish in one gulp.
Do the calculations for many mouthfuls!

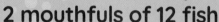

2 mouthfuls of 12 fish

12 + 12 = ☐   2 x 12 = ☐

4 mouthfuls of 12 fish

12 + 12 + 12 + 12 = ☐   4 x 12 = ☐

5 mouthfuls of 12 fish

12 + 12 + 12 + 12 + 12 = ☐   5 x 12 = ☐

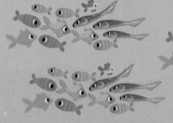    

7 mouthfuls of 12 fish

 12 + 12 + 12 + 12 + 12 + 12 + 12 = ☐

7 x 12 = ☐

Numbersaurus

First, solve each sum and write the answer on the dot.
Next, follow the key to shade in the dinosaurs.

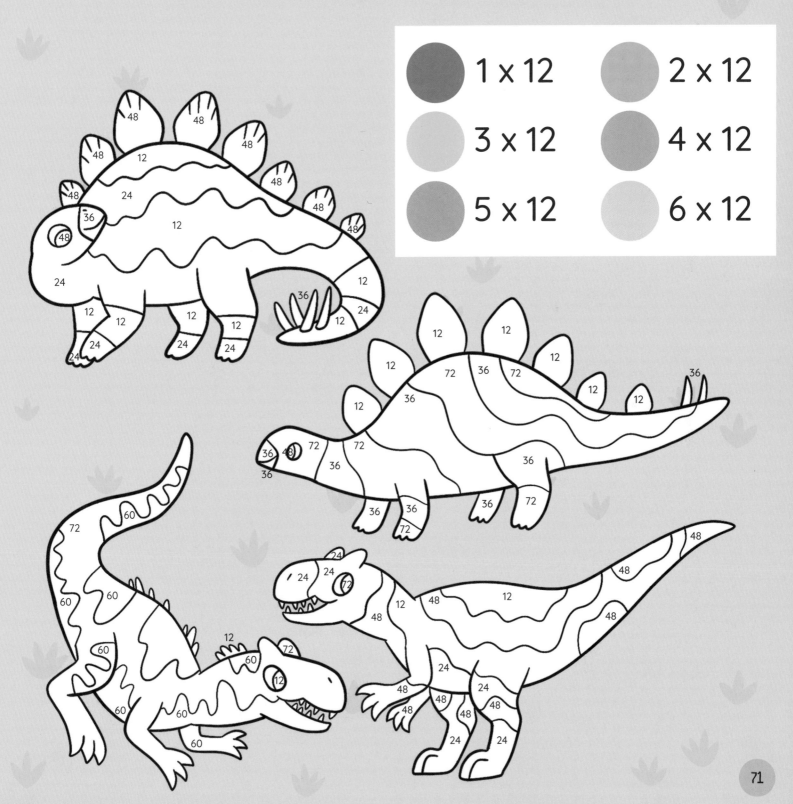

1 x 12

2 x 12

3 x 12

4 x 12

5 x 12

6 x 12

Twelve times table

Twelve snails can climb onto Priti the Protoceratops' back.
How many can she carry if she does several trips?

1 x 12 =

2 x 12 =

3 x 12 =

4 x 12 =

5 x 12 =

6 x 12 =

7 x 12 =

8 x 12 =

9 x 12 =

10 x 12 =

11 x 12 =

12 x 12 =

Missing numbers

Help the Spinosaurus friends fill in the missing numbers from the 12 times table.

1 x ☐ = 12

☐ x 12 = 24

☐ x 12 = 60

3 x 12 = ☐

6 x ☐ = 72

☐ x 12 = 120

11 x 12 = ☐

8 x 12 = ☐

☐ x 12 = 48

☐ x 12 = 108

7 x 12 = ☐

12 x 12 = ☐

73

Spiky twelves

Help each Kentrosaurus to find a partner by solving the problems and matching them into pairs.

24

4 x 12

84

96

2 x 12

48

7 x 12

8 x 12

72

36

60

6 x 12

3 x 12

5 x 12

Caught in a trap

Write in the missing numbers by multiplying the spider numbers by the web numbers. The first one has been done for you.

Times table test

Put your knowledge to the test by doing these calculations, using all of the times tables that you have learned.

6 x 9 =

7 x 5 =

5 x 8 =

4 x 3 =

10 x 4 =

6 x 6 =

7 x 2 =

7 x 10 =

6 x 8 =

5 x 4 =

7 x 9 =

7 x 6 =

8 x 10 =

2 x 12 =

8 x 7 = ☐

7 x 12 = ☐

4 x 4 = ☐

9 x 3 = ☐

6 x 5 = ☐

8 x 5 = ☐

6 x 10 = ☐

6 x 4 = ☐

9 x 2 = ☐

5 x 7 = ☐

3 x 11 = ☐

8 x 2 = ☐

9 x 10 = ☐

4 x 11 = ☐

Drinking dinos

Each dinosaur is worth a different amount. If they gather at the watering hole on two days, work out the points value for each day.

6

3

10

8

DAY 1

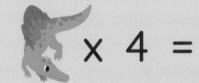 x 3 =

x 5 =

x 7 =

x 7 =

Total for Day 1 =

DAY 2

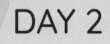 x 6 =

x 4 =

x 5 =

x 3 =

Total for Day 2 =

Prehistoric pond

Match each of the frogs to the correct answer on the pond.

4 x 6

18

50

7 x 5

36

24

9 x 2

10 x 5

21

6 x 6

35

3 x 7

Missing numbers

Several calculations give the same answer.
Fill in the missing numbers for these.

☐ x 4 = 20

☐ x 5 = 20

☐ x 2 = 20

☐ x 10 = 20

☐ x 6 = 24

☐ x 4 = 24

☐ x 12 = 24

☐ x 2 = 24

☐ x 8 = 24

☐ x 3 = 24

☐ x 4 = 36

☐ x 9 = 36

☐ x 6 = 36

☐ x 12 = 36

☐ x 3 = 36

☐ x 5 = 60

☐ x 12 = 60

☐ x 10 = 60

☐ x 6 = 60

Inverse relationships

If you know a multiplication fact, you can work out two related division facts. Finish the ones shown here.

$$9 \times 2 = 18$$

$$18 \div 9 = 2$$

$$18 \div 2 = 9$$

$$10 \times 3 = 30$$

$$30 \div 10 = \boxed{}$$

$$30 \div 3 = \boxed{}$$

$$4 \times 8 = 32$$

$$32 \div 4 = \boxed{}$$

$$32 \div 8 = \boxed{}$$

$$5 \times 7 = 35$$

$$35 \div 5 = \boxed{}$$

$$35 \div 7 = \boxed{}$$

$$6 \times 9 = 54$$

$$54 \div 6 = \boxed{}$$

$$54 \div 9 = \boxed{}$$

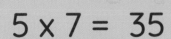

Three of clubs

Each of the club-tailed Euoplocephalus has three numbers. Follow the example to write down the multiplication and division facts for each one. The first one has been done for you.

16
8
2

8	x	2	=	16
2	x	8	=	16
16	÷	2	=	8
16	÷	8	=	2

80
10
8

	x		=	
	x		=	
	÷		=	
	÷		=	

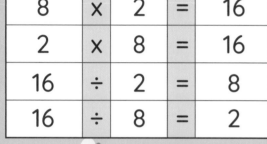

60
5
12

	x		=	
	x		=	
	÷		=	
	÷		=	

28
7
4

	x		=	
	x		=	
	÷		=	
	÷		=	

With multiplication, it doesn't matter which way round the numbers go, but it does matter with division, because the order affects what answer you get.

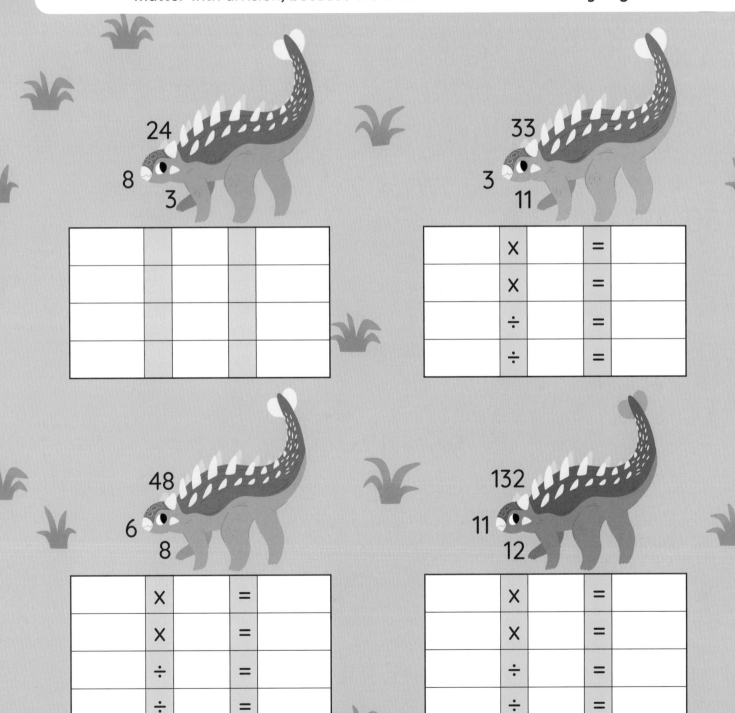

24
8
3

33
3
11

		×		=	
		×		=	
		÷		=	
		÷		=	

48
6
8

132
11
12

	×		=	
	×		=	
	÷		=	
	÷		=	

	×		=	
	×		=	
	÷		=	
	÷		=	

Odd one out

Pair up the calculations that have the same answer.
Which calculation has no match?

3 x 3

56 ÷ 8

70 ÷ 7

60 ÷ 5

54 ÷ 6

12 x 2

2 x 5

96 ÷ 12

2 x 6

8 x 3

14 ÷ 2

Looking for the one

Find a dinosaur that has a calculation that gives the answer 12.

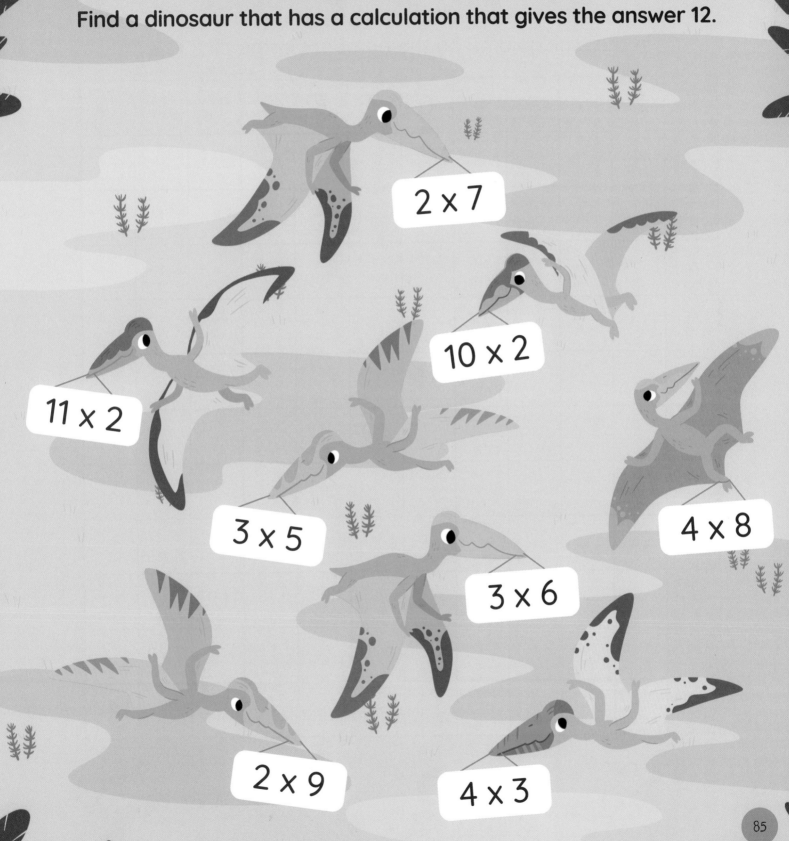

2 x 7

10 x 2

11 x 2

3 x 5

4 x 8

3 x 6

2 x 9

4 x 3

Times table grid

Complete the grid by multiplying the numbers
in the pink column by the numbers in the pink row.

1	2	3	4	5	6	7	8	9	10	11	12
2	4										
3		9									
4			16								
5				25							
6					36						
7						49					
8							64				
9								81			
10									100		
11										121	
12											144

Answers

4 Groups of two

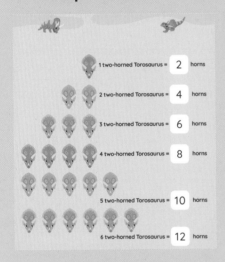

1 two-horned Torosaurus = **2** horns

2 two-horned Torosaurus = **4** horns

3 two-horned Torosaurus = **6** horns

4 two-horned Torosaurus = **8** horns

5 two-horned Torosaurus = **10** horns

6 two-horned Torosaurus = **12** horns

5 More twos

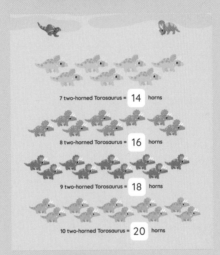

7 two-horned Torosaurus = **14** horns

8 two-horned Torosaurus = **16** horns

9 two-horned Torosaurus = **18** horns

10 two-horned Torosaurus = **20** horns

6 Repeated addition

2 + 2 + 2 = **6**   2 + 2 + 2 + 2 = **8**

3 x 2 = **6**   4 x 2 = **8**

2 + 2 = **4**   2 + 2 + 2 + 2 + 2 + 2 = **12**

2 x 2 = **4**   6 x 2 = **12**

7 Match up

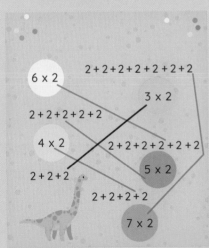

6 x 2 — 2 + 2 + 2 + 2 + 2 + 2

3 x 2

2 + 2 + 2 + 2 + 2

4 x 2

2 + 2 + 2 + 2 + 2 + 2

2 + 2 + 2

5 x 2

2 + 2 + 2 + 2

7 x 2

8 Number lines

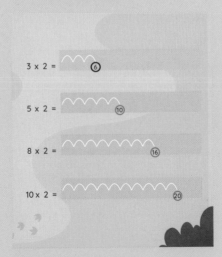

3 x 2 = ⑥

5 x 2 = ⑩

8 x 2 = ⑯

10 x 2 = ⑳

q Rock hoppers

10 Two times table

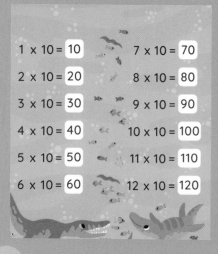

1 x 2 = 2	7 x 2 = 14
2 x 2 = 4	8 x 2 = 16
3 x 2 = 6	9 x 2 = 18
4 x 2 = 8	10 x 2 = 20
5 x 2 = 10	11 x 2 = 22
6 x 2 = 12	12 x 2 = 24

11 Missing numbers

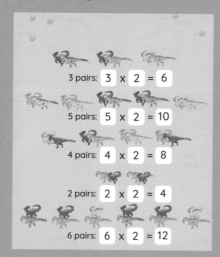

3 pairs: 3 x 2 = 6

5 pairs: 5 x 2 = 10

4 pairs: 4 x 2 = 8

2 pairs: 2 x 2 = 4

6 pairs: 6 x 2 = 12

12 Matching multiples

6   12 x 2   6 x 2
8 x 2   14
3 x 2   11 x 2
18   4 x 2
16   9 x 2
24   7 x 2   12
22   8

13 What's missing?

3 x 2 = 6	8 x 2 = 16
7 x 2 = 14	1 x 2 = 2
5 x 2 = 10	9 x 2 = 18
10 x 2 = 20	2 x 2 = 4
4 x 2 = 8	6 x 2 = 12

14 Groups of ten

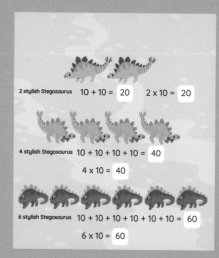

2 stylish Stegosaurus   10 + 10 = 20   2 x 10 = 20

4 stylish Stegosaurus   10 + 10 + 10 + 10 = 40

4 x 10 = 40

6 stylish Stegosaurus   10 + 10 + 10 + 10 + 10 + 10 = 60

6 x 10 = 60

15 More fossils

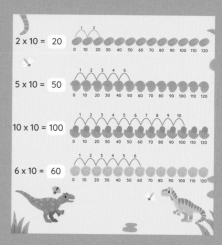

2 x 10 = 20

5 x 10 = 50

10 x 10 = 100

6 x 10 = 60

16 Ten times table

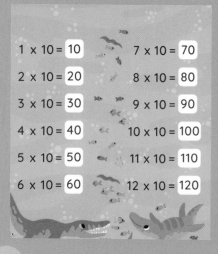

1 x 10 = 10	7 x 10 = 70
2 x 10 = 20	8 x 10 = 80
3 x 10 = 30	9 x 10 = 90
4 x 10 = 40	10 x 10 = 100
5 x 10 = 50	11 x 10 = 110
6 x 10 = 60	12 x 10 = 120

17 Missing numbers

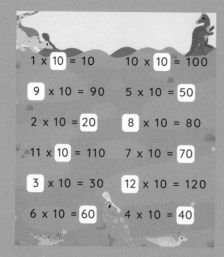

1 x 10 = 10	10 x 10 = 100
9 x 10 = 90	5 x 10 = 50
2 x 10 = 20	8 x 10 = 80
11 x 10 = 110	7 x 10 = 70
3 x 10 = 30	12 x 10 = 120
6 x 10 = 60	4 x 10 = 40

18 Heads and tails

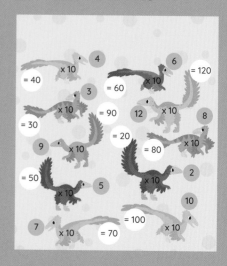

4   6
x 10   x 10   = 120
= 40
3   = 60
x 10   = 90   12   x 10   8
= 30   = 20
9   x 10   = 80
= 50   x 10
7   5   x 10   2
x 10   = 100   x 10   10
= 70

19 Flying high

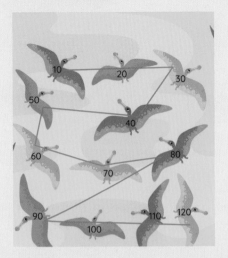

20 Dot to dot

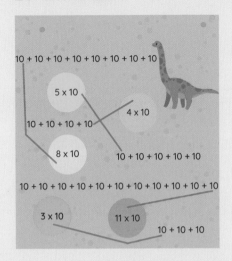

21 Pick a partner

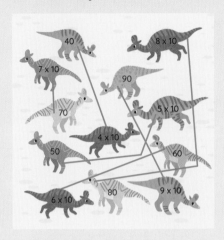

22 Groups of five

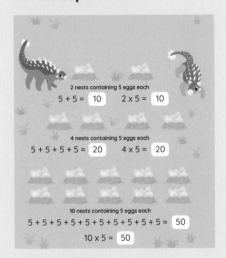

2 nests containing 5 eggs each
5 + 5 = 10   2 x 5 = 10

4 nests containing 5 eggs each
5 + 5 + 5 + 5 = 20   4 x 5 = 20

10 nests containing 5 eggs each
5 + 5 + 5 + 5 + 5 + 5 + 5 + 5 + 5 + 5 = 50
10 x 5 = 50

23 Even dinos love their toys

24 Five times table

1 x 5 = 5   7 x 5 = 35
2 x 5 = 10   8 x 5 = 40
3 x 5 = 15   9 x 5 = 45
4 x 5 = 20   10 x 5 = 50
5 x 5 = 25   11 x 5 = 55
6 x 5 = 30   12 x 5 = 60

25 Missing numbers

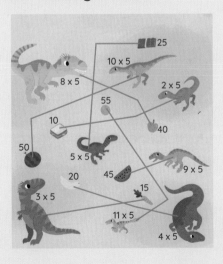

26 Forgetful fives

5 x 5 = 25   8 x 5 = 40

1 x 5 = 5   7 x 5 = 35

6 x 5 = 30   11 x 5 = 55

10 x 5 = 50   9 x 5 = 45

2 x 5 = 10   4 x 5 = 20

3 x 5 = 15   12 x 5 = 60

27 High five

1 x 5 = 5   7 x 5 = 35
2 x 5 = 10   8 x 5 = 40
3 x 5 = 15   9 x 5 = 45
4 x 5 = 20   10 x 5 = 50
5 x 5 = 25   11 x 5 = 55
6 x 5 = 30   12 x 5 = 60

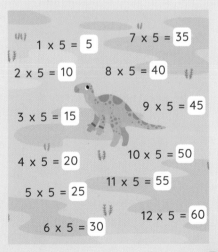

89

28 Groups of four

2 dinosaurs pick 4 flowers each
4 + 4 = 8   2 x 4 = 8

3 dinosaurs pick 4 flowers each
4 + 4 + 4 = 12   3 x 4 = 12

5 dinosaurs pick 4 flowers each
4 + 4 + 4 + 4 + 4 = 20
5 x 4 = 20

29 Darting dragonflies

4
12   8
16
20
24
28   32

30 Four times table

1 x 4 = 4		7 x 4 = 28	
2 x 4 = 8		8 x 4 = 32	
3 x 4 = 12		9 x 4 = 36	
4 x 4 = 16		10 x 4 = 40	
5 x 4 = 20		11 x 4 = 44	
6 x 4 = 24		12 x 4 = 48	

31 Missing numbers

6 x 4 = 24	11 x 4 = 44
10 x 4 = 40	7 x 4 = 28
4 x 4 = 16	5 x 4 = 20
9 x 4 = 36	8 x 4 = 32
1 x 4 = 4	3 x 4 = 12
2 x 4 = 8	12 x 4 = 48

32 Deep thinkers

4 x 4 =   7 x 4 =
16   28
5 x 4 = 20   9 x 4 = 36
10 x 4 = 40   3 x 4 = 12

33 Something's wrong

16
12
8
48
20   22
4   32

34 Groups of eight

2 mouthfuls of 8 leaves
8 + 8 = 16   2 x 8 = 16

3 mouthfuls of 8 leaves
8 + 8 + 8 = 24   3 x 8 = 24

5 mouthfuls of 8 leaves
8 + 8 + 8 + 8 + 8 = 40   5 x 8 = 40

9 mouthfuls of 8 leaves
8 + 8 + 8 + 8 + 8 + 8 + 8 + 8 + 8 = 72
9 x 8 = 72

35 Lost and found

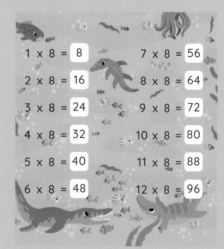

8
16   32
24
40
48   72
64
56   80

36 Eight times table

1 x 8 = 8		7 x 8 = 56	
2 x 8 = 16		8 x 8 = 64	
3 x 8 = 24		9 x 8 = 72	
4 x 8 = 32		10 x 8 = 80	
5 x 8 = 40		11 x 8 = 88	
6 x 8 = 48		12 x 8 = 96	

37 Missing numbers

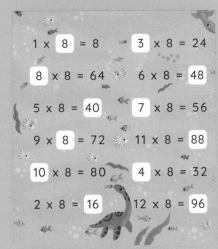

1 x **8** = 8   **3** x 8 = 24

8 x 8 = 64   6 x 8 = **48**

5 x 8 = **40**   **7** x 8 = 56

9 x **8** = 72   11 x 8 = **88**

10 x 8 = 80   **4** x 8 = 32

2 x 8 = **16**   12 x 8 = **96**

38 Broom broom!

39 Crazy creatures

8 1 x 8
16 2 x 8
24 3 x 8
32 4 x 8
40 5 x 8
48 6 x 8

40 Groups of three

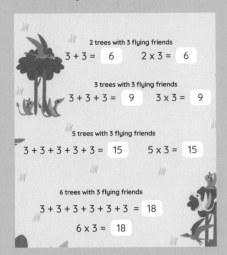

2 trees with 3 flying friends
3 + 3 = **6**   2 x 3 = **6**

3 trees with 3 flying friends
3 + 3 + 3 = **9**   3 x 3 = **9**

5 trees with 3 flying friends
3 + 3 + 3 + 3 + 3 = **15**   5 x 3 = **15**

6 trees with 3 flying friends
3 + 3 + 3 + 3 + 3 + 3 = **18**
6 x 3 = **18**

41 Forest trail

42 Three times table

1 x 3 = **3**   7 x 3 = 21

2 x 3 = **6**   8 x 3 = 24

3 x 3 = **9**   9 x 3 = 27

4 x 3 = **12**   10 x 3 = 30

5 x 3 = **15**   11 x 3 = 33

6 x 3 = **18**   12 x 3 = 36

43 Missing numbers

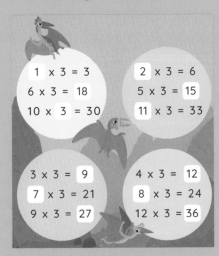

1 x 3 = 3   2 x 3 = 6
6 x 3 = **18**   5 x 3 = **15**
10 x **3** = 30   11 x 3 = 33

3 x 3 = **9**   4 x 3 = **12**
7 x 3 = **21**   8 x 3 = 24
9 x 3 = **27**   12 x 3 = **36**

44 Heads and tails

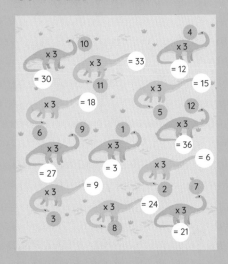

45 Starfall

91

46 Groups of six

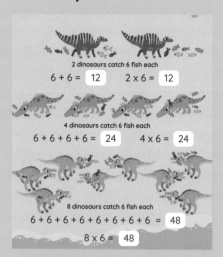

2 dinosaurs catch 6 fish each

6 + 6 = 12   2 x 6 = 12

4 dinosaurs catch 6 fish each

6 + 6 + 6 + 6 = 24   4 x 6 = 24

8 dinosaurs catch 6 fish each

6 + 6 + 6 + 6 + 6 + 6 + 6 + 6 = 48

8 x 6 = 48

47 All the sixes

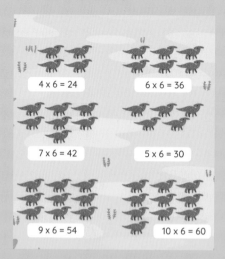

4 x 6 = 24   6 x 6 = 36

7 x 6 = 42   5 x 6 = 30

9 x 6 = 54   10 x 6 = 60

48 Six times table

1 x 6 = 6	7 x 6 = 42
2 x 6 = 12	8 x 6 = 48
3 x 6 = 18	9 x 6 = 54
4 x 6 = 24	10 x 6 = 60
5 x 6 = 30	11 x 6 = 66
6 x 6 = 36	12 x 6 = 72

49 Number square

1	2	3	4	5	6	7	8	9	10
11	12	13	14	15	16	17	18	19	20
21	22	23	24	25	26	27	28	29	30
31	32	33	34	35	36	37	38	39	40
41	42	43	44	45	46	47	48	49	50
51	52	53	54	55	56	57	58	59	60
61	62	63	64	65	66	67	68	69	70
71	72	73	74	75	76	77	78	79	80
81	82	83	84	85	86	87	88	89	90
91	92	93	94	95	96	97	98	99	100

50 Missing numbers

1 x 6 = 6	11 x 6 = 66
6 x 6 = 36	9 x 6 = 54
4 x 6 = 24	7 x 6 = 42
10 x 6 = 60	2 x 6 = 12
5 x 6 = 30	3 x 6 = 18
8 x 6 = 48	12 x 6 = 72

51 Find a friend

52 Groups of nine

2 groups of 9 worms

9 + 9 = 18   2 x 9 = 18

4 groups of 9 worms

9 + 9 + 9 + 9 = 36   4 x 9 = 36

5 groups of 9 worms

9 + 9 + 9 + 9 + 9 = 45   5 x 9 = 45

53 Down in the deep

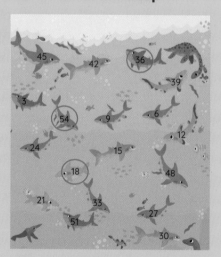

54 Nine times table

1 x 9 = 9	7 x 9 = 63
2 x 9 = 18	8 x 9 = 72
3 x 9 = 27	9 x 9 = 81
4 x 9 = 36	10 x 9 = 90
5 x 9 = 45	11 x 9 = 99
6 x 9 = 54	12 x 9 = 108

55 Missing numbers

1 x **9** = 9   6 x 9 = **54**

2 x 9 = **18**   **8** x 9 = 72

9 x 9 = 81   11 x 9 = **99**

7 x 9 = **63**   **4** x 9 = 36

10 x **9** = 90   5 x 9 = **45**

3 x 9 = 27   12 x 9 = **108**

56 Newborns

36   3 x 9   18

2 x 9   81   5 x 9

63

54   7 x 9   8 x 9

72   9 x 9   45

4 x 9   6 x 9   27

57 Number square

1	2	3	4	5	6	7	8	9	10
11	12	13	14	15	16	17	18	19	20
21	22	23	24	25	26	27	28	29	30
31	32	33	34	35	36	37	38	39	40
41	42	43	44	45	46	47	48	49	50
51	52	53	54	55	56	57	58	59	60
61	62	63	64	65	66	67	68	69	70
71	72	73	74	75	76	77	78	79	80
81	82	83	84	85	86	87	88	89	90
91	92	93	94	95	96	97	98	99	100

58 Groups of seven

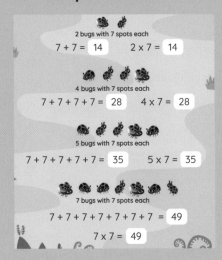

2 bugs with 7 spots each
7 + 7 = **14**   2 x 7 = **14**

4 bugs with 7 spots each
7 + 7 + 7 + 7 = **28**   4 x 7 = **28**

5 bugs with 7 spots each
7 + 7 + 7 + 7 + 7 = **35**   5 x 7 = **35**

7 bugs with 7 spots each
7 + 7 + 7 + 7 + 7 + 7 + 7 = **49**

7 x 7 = **49**

59 Off we go!

35   28

14   42

21   84

60 Seven times table

1 x 7 = **7**   7 x 7 = **49**

2 x 7 = **14**   8 x 7 = **56**

3 x 7 = **21**   9 x 7 = **63**

4 x 7 = **28**   10 x 7 = **70**

5 x 7 = **35**   11 x 7 = **77**

6 x 7 = **42**   12 x 7 = **84**

61 Missing numbers

1 x **7** = 7   **3** x 7 = 21

10 x 7 = **70**   6 x 7 = **42**

2 x 7 = 14   **8** x 7 = 56

11 x **7** = 77   4 x 7 = **28**

5 x 7 = 35   **12** x 7 = 84

9 x 7 = **63**   7 x 7 = **49**

62 Spots and stripes

8 x 7   12 x 7

84

5 x 7   4 x 7

21   63

6 x 7   35   42   9 x 7

14   56

2 x 7   3 x 7   28

63 Black and white

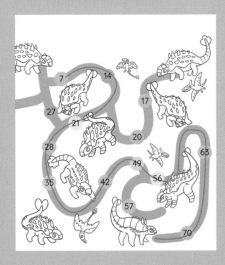

7   14

17

27

21   20

28

49   63

35   42   56

57

70

93

64 Groups of eleven

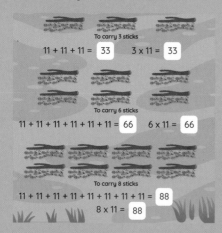

To carry 3 sticks
11 + 11 + 11 = 33   3 x 11 = 33

To carry 6 sticks
11 + 11 + 11 + 11 + 11 + 11 = 66   6 x 11 = 66

To carry 8 sticks
11 + 11 + 11 + 11 + 11 + 11 + 11 + 11 = 88
8 x 11 = 88

65 All the elevens

88
55
110
11
22
132
122
77
66
44
99
121
33

66 Eleven times table

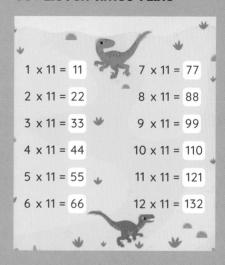

1 x 11 = 11	7 x 11 = 77
2 x 11 = 22	8 x 11 = 88
3 x 11 = 33	9 x 11 = 99
4 x 11 = 44	10 x 11 = 110
5 x 11 = 55	11 x 11 = 121
6 x 11 = 66	12 x 11 = 132

67 Missing numbers

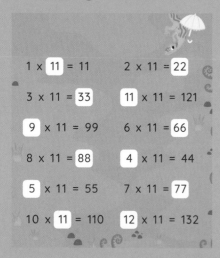

1 x 11 = 11	2 x 11 = 22
3 x 11 = 33	11 x 11 = 121
9 x 11 = 99	6 x 11 = 66
8 x 11 = 88	4 x 11 = 44
5 x 11 = 55	7 x 11 = 77
10 x 11 = 110	12 x 11 = 132

68 Practice makes perfect

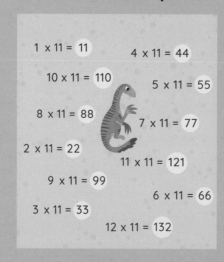

1 x 11 = 11
4 x 11 = 44
10 x 11 = 110
5 x 11 = 55
8 x 11 = 88
7 x 11 = 77
2 x 11 = 22
11 x 11 = 121
9 x 11 = 99
6 x 11 = 66
3 x 11 = 33
12 x 11 = 132

69 Fancy footwear

77   7 x 11   99
9 x 11
12 x 11
132
5 x 11
55
10 x 11   110
88
8 x 11
11 x 11   6 x 11
121   66

70 Groups of twelve

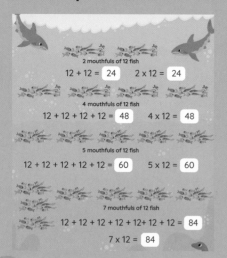

2 mouthfuls of 12 fish
12 + 12 = 24   2 x 12 = 24

4 mouthfuls of 12 fish
12 + 12 + 12 + 12 = 48   4 x 12 = 48

5 mouthfuls of 12 fish
12 + 12 + 12 + 12 + 12 = 60   5 x 12 = 60

7 mouthfuls of 12 fish
12 + 12 + 12 + 12 + 12 + 12 + 12 = 84
7 x 12 = 84

71 Numbersaurus

12	1 x 12	24	2 x 12
36	3 x 12	48	4 x 12
60	5 x 12	72	6 x 12

72 Twelve times table

1 x 12 = 12	7 x 12 = 84
2 x 12 = 24	8 x 12 = 96
3 x 12 = 36	9 x 12 = 108
4 x 12 = 48	10 x 12 = 120
5 x 12 = 60	11 x 12 = 132
6 x 12 = 72	12 x 12 = 144

73 Missing numbers

1 x **12** = 12   **2** x 12 = 24

5 x 12 = 60   3 x 12 = **36**

6 x **12** = 72   10 x 12 = 120

11 x 12 = **132**   8 x 12 = **96**

4 x 12 = 48   **9** x 12 = 108

7 x 12 = **84**   12 x 12 = **144**

74 Spiky twelves

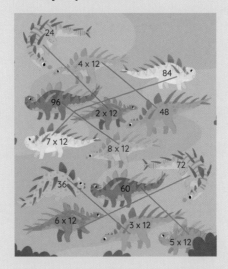

24
4 x 12
84
96
2 x 12   48
7 x 12
8 x 12
72
36   60
6 x 12
3 x 12
5 x 12

75 Caught in a trap

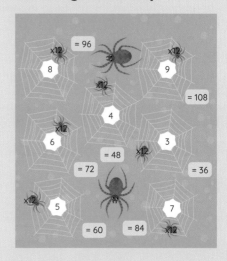

= 96
x12   x12
8   **9**
x12
= 108
4
x12
6   **3**
= 48   x12
= 72   = 36
x12
5   **7**
= 60   = 84   x12

76 Times table test

6 x 9 = **54**   7 x 5 = **35**

5 x 8 = **40**   4 x 3 = **12**

10 x 4 = **40**   6 x 6 = **36**

7 x 2 = **14**   7 x 10 = **70**

6 x 8 = **48**   5 x 4 = **20**

7 x 9 = **63**   7 x 6 = **42**

8 x 10 = **80**   2 x 12 = **24**

77 Times table test continued

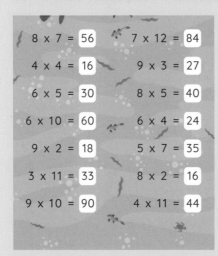

8 x 7 = **56**   7 x 12 = **84**

4 x 4 = **16**   9 x 3 = **27**

6 x 5 = **30**   8 x 5 = **40**

6 x 10 = **60**   6 x 4 = **24**

9 x 2 = **18**   5 x 7 = **35**

3 x 11 = **33**   8 x 2 = **16**

9 x 10 = **90**   4 x 11 = **44**

78 Drinking dinos

6   3
10
8
DAY 1   DAY 2

x 3 = **30**   x 6 = **18**

x 5 = **15**   x 4 = **24**

x 7 = **56**   x 5 = **50**

x 7 = **42**   x 3 = **24**

Total for Day 1 = **143**   Total for Day 2 = **116**

79 Prehistoric pond

4 x 6   18
7 x 5   36   50
24   9 x 2   10 x 5
21   6 x 6   35
3 x 7

80 Missing numbers

5 x 4 = 20   **4** x 6 = 24

4 x 5 = 20   **6** x 4 = 24

10 x 2 = 20   **2** x 12 = 24

2 x 10 = 20   **12** x 2 = 24

                        3 x 8 = 24

                        8 x 3 = 24

9 x 4 = 36

4 x 9 = 36   **12** x 5 = 60

6 x 6 = 36   **5** x 12 = 60

3 x 12 = 36   **6** x 10 = 60

12 x 3 = 36   **10** x 6 = 60

81 Inverse relationships

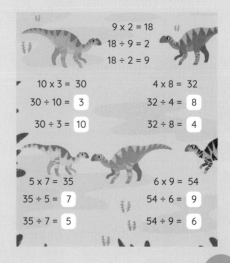

9 x 2 = 18
18 ÷ 9 = 2
18 ÷ 2 = 9

10 x 3 = 30   4 x 8 = 32
30 ÷ 10 = **3**   32 ÷ 4 = **8**
30 ÷ 3 = **10**   32 ÷ 8 = **4**

5 x 7 = 35   6 x 9 = 54
35 ÷ 5 = **7**   54 ÷ 6 = **9**
35 ÷ 7 = **5**   54 ÷ 9 = **6**

82 Three of clubs

8	x	2	=	16
2	x	8	=	16
16	÷	2	=	8
16	÷	8	=	2

10	x	8	=	80
8	x	10	=	80
80	÷	8	=	10
80	÷	10	=	8

5	x	12	=	60
12	x	5	=	60
60	÷	12	=	5
60	÷	5	=	12

7	x	4	=	28
4	x	7	=	28
28	÷	4	=	7
28	÷	7	=	4

83 Three of clubs continued

8	x	3	=	24
3	x	8	=	24
24	÷	3	=	8
24	÷	8	=	3

3	x	11	=	33
11	x	3	=	33
33	÷	11	=	3
33	÷	3	=	11

6	x	8	=	48
8	x	6	=	48
48	÷	8	=	6
48	÷	6	=	8

11	x	12	=	132
12	x	11	=	132
132	÷	12	=	11
132	÷	11	=	12

84 Odd one out

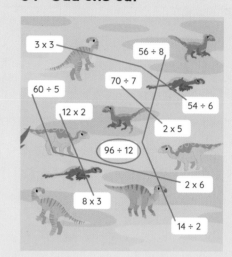

3 x 3 56 ÷ 8 70 ÷ 7 60 ÷ 5 54 ÷ 6 12 x 2 2 x 5 96 ÷ 12 2 x 6 8 x 3 14 ÷ 2

85 Looking for the one

2 x 7 10 x 2 11 x 2 3 x 5 4 x 8 3 x 6 2 x 9 4 x 3

86 Times table grid

1	2	3	4	5	6	7	8	9	10	11	12
2	4	6	8	10	12	14	16	18	20	22	24
3	6	9	12	15	18	21	24	27	30	33	36
4	8	12	16	20	24	28	32	36	40	44	48
5	10	15	20	25	30	35	40	45	50	55	60
6	12	18	24	30	36	42	48	54	60	66	72
7	14	21	28	35	42	49	56	63	70	77	84
8	16	24	32	40	48	56	64	72	80	88	96
9	18	27	36	45	54	63	72	81	90	99	108
10	20	30	40	50	60	70	80	90	100	110	120
11	22	33	44	55	66	77	88	99	110	121	132
12	24	36	48	60	72	84	96	108	120	132	144